THINGS
I WANT TO SAY
AT WORK
BUT CAN'T

Oh! there's one more thing

You're a C*nt

WELL F*CK ME BACKWARDS WITH A TELEGRAPH POLE

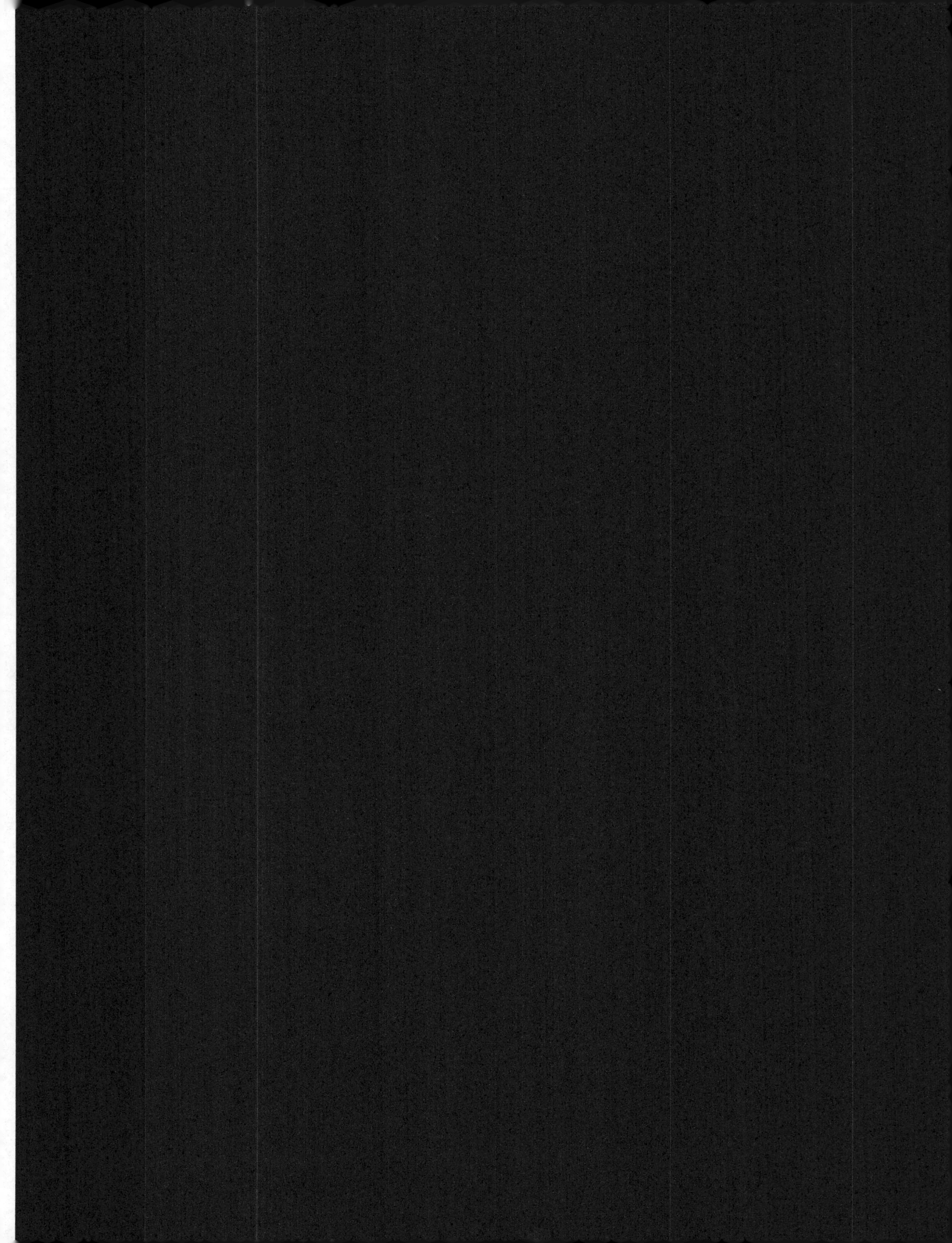

I like people i work with generally, With Four Exceptions.

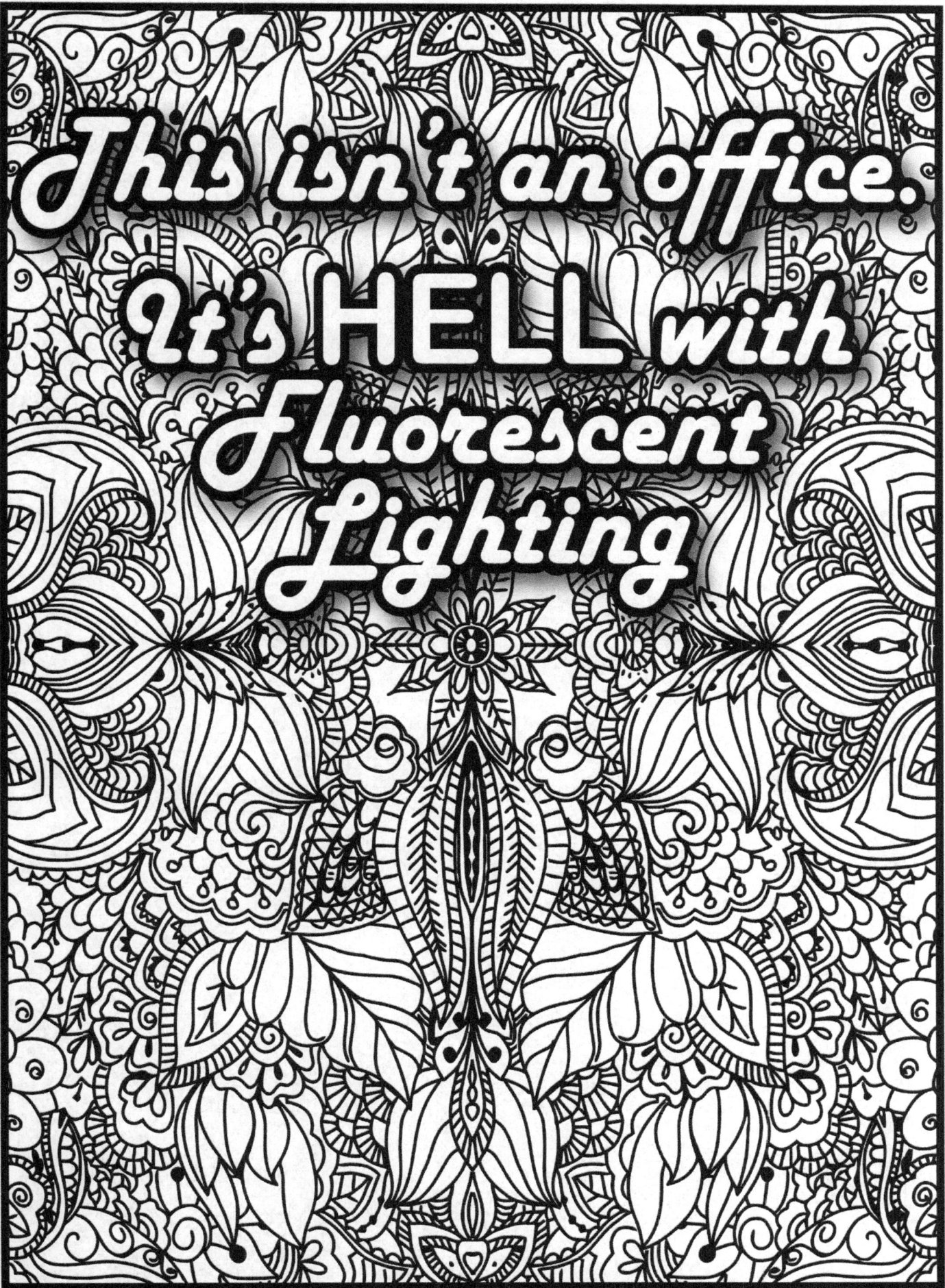

This isn't an office. It's HELL with Fluorescent Lighting

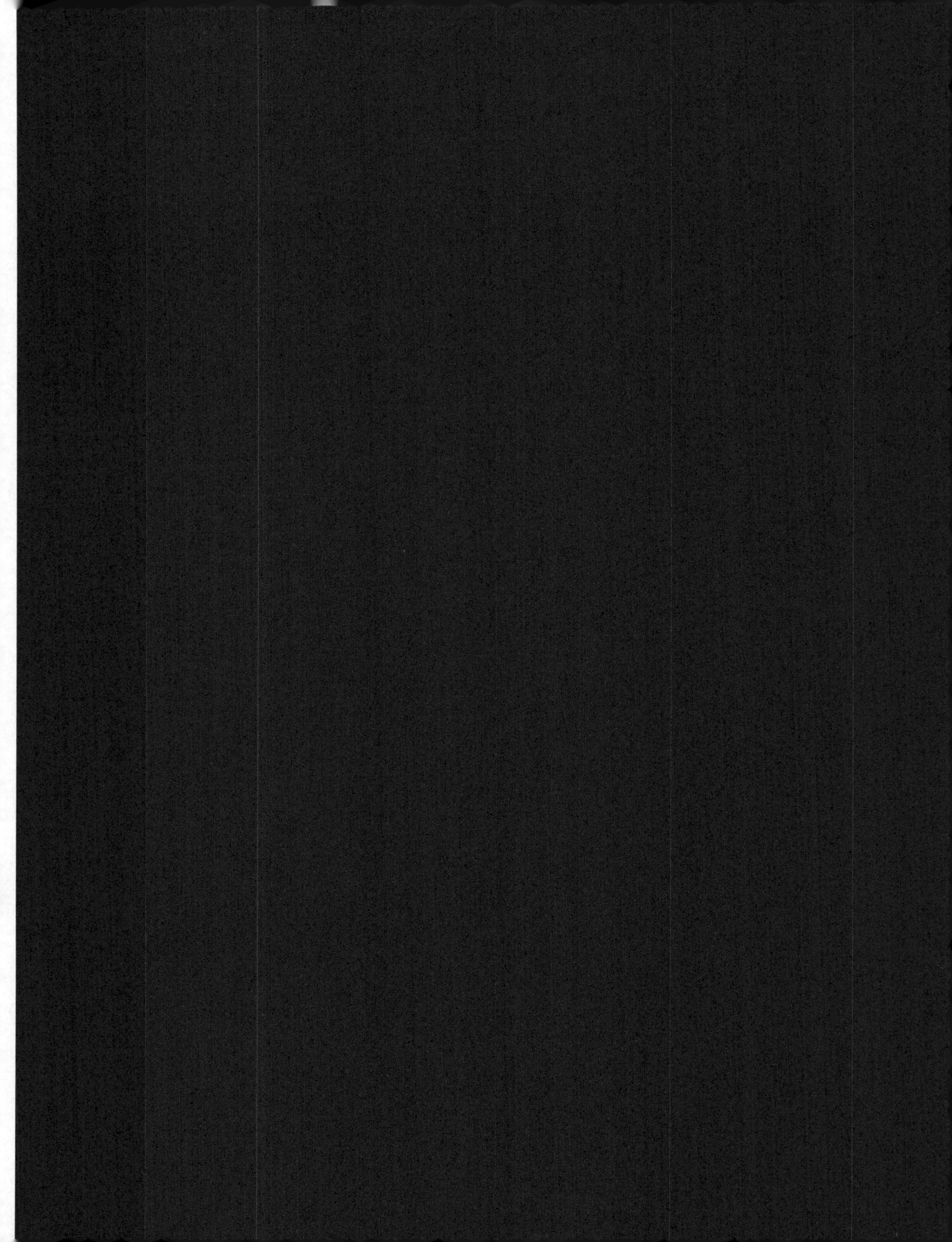

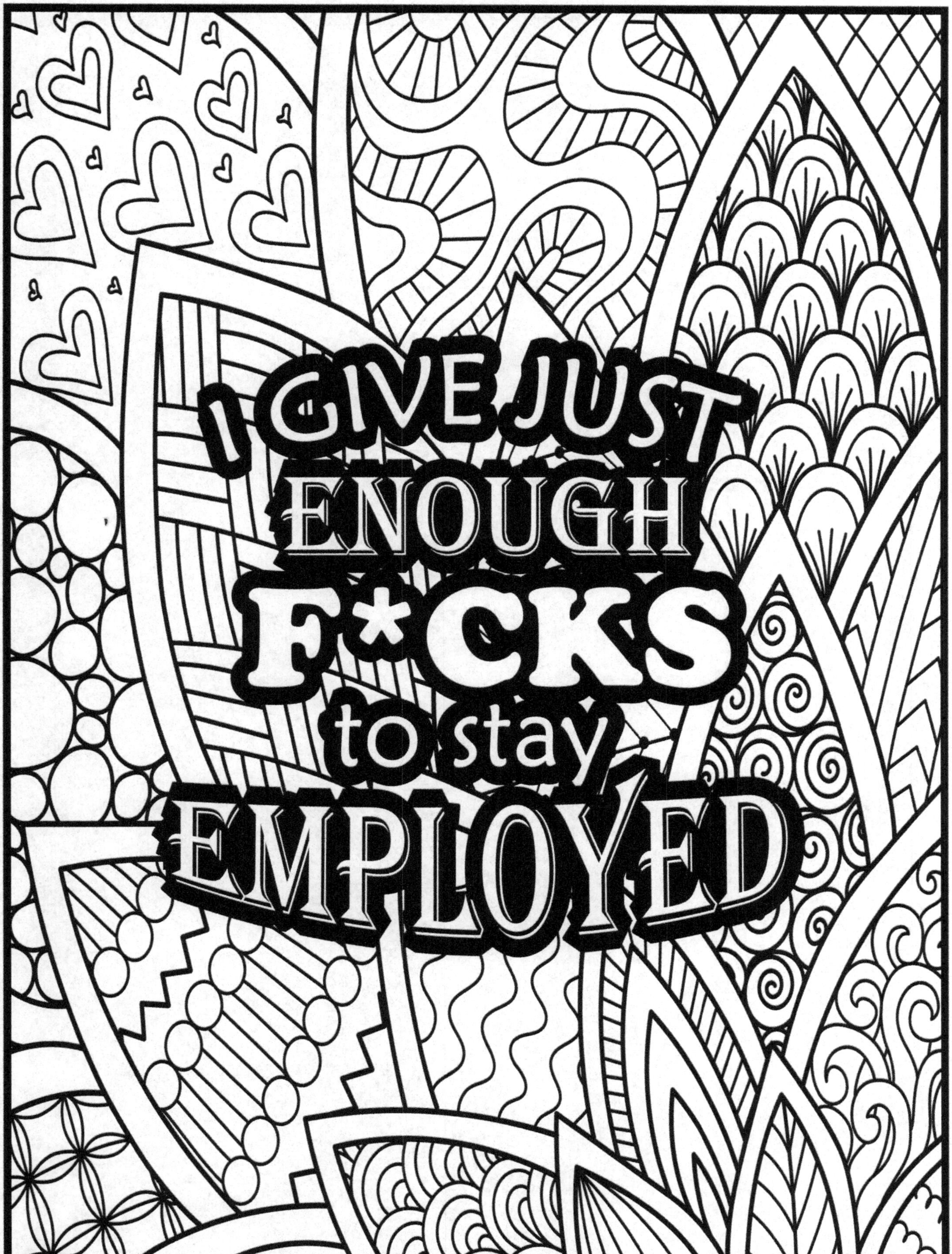
I GIVE JUST
ENOUGH
F*CKS
to stay
EMPLOYED

Let me file THAT UNDER I don't give a SH*T

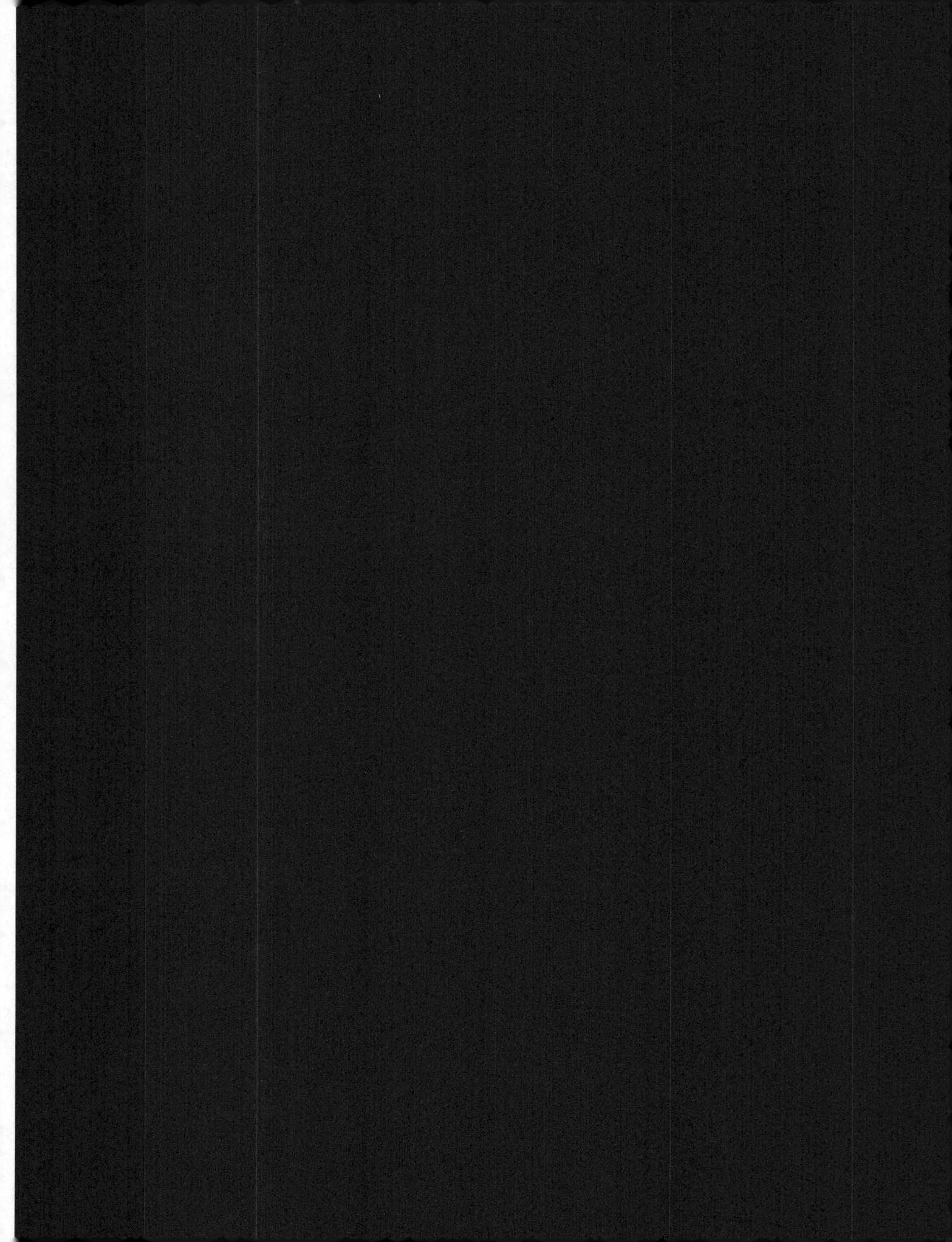

TOO MANY FREAKS NOT ENOUGH CIRCUSES

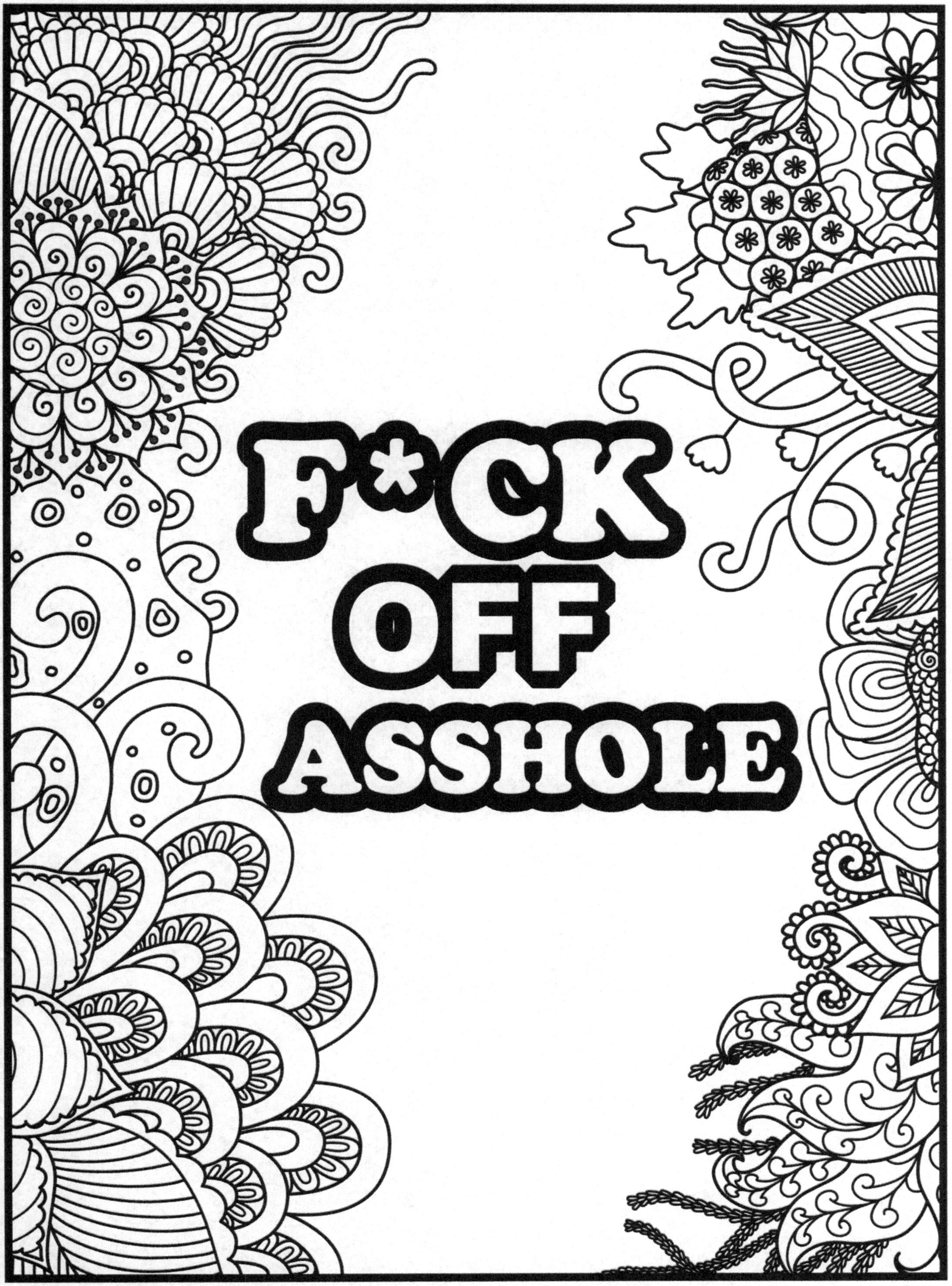
F*CK
OFF
ASSHOLE

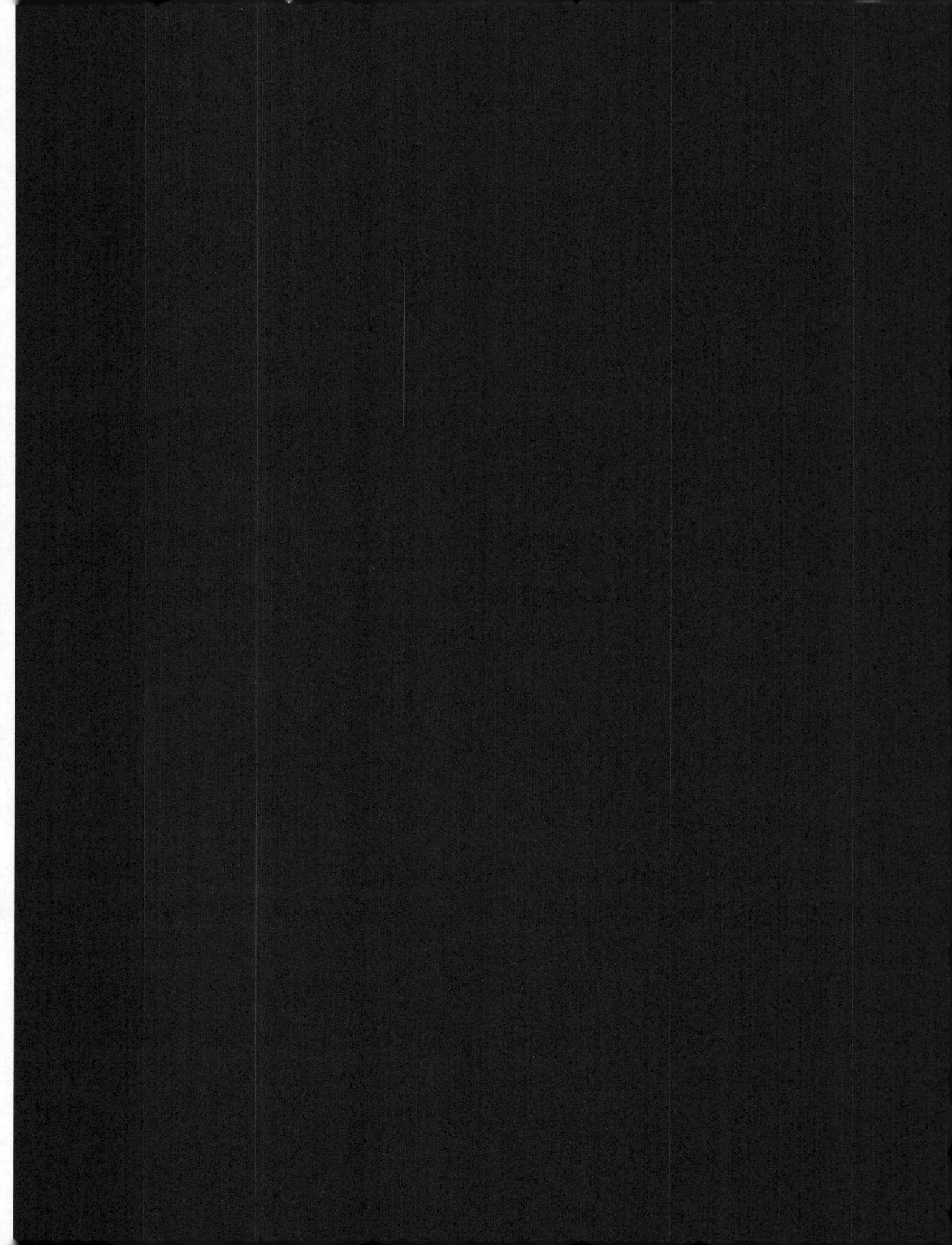

HERE WE F*CKING GO AGAIN... I MEAN GOODMORNING

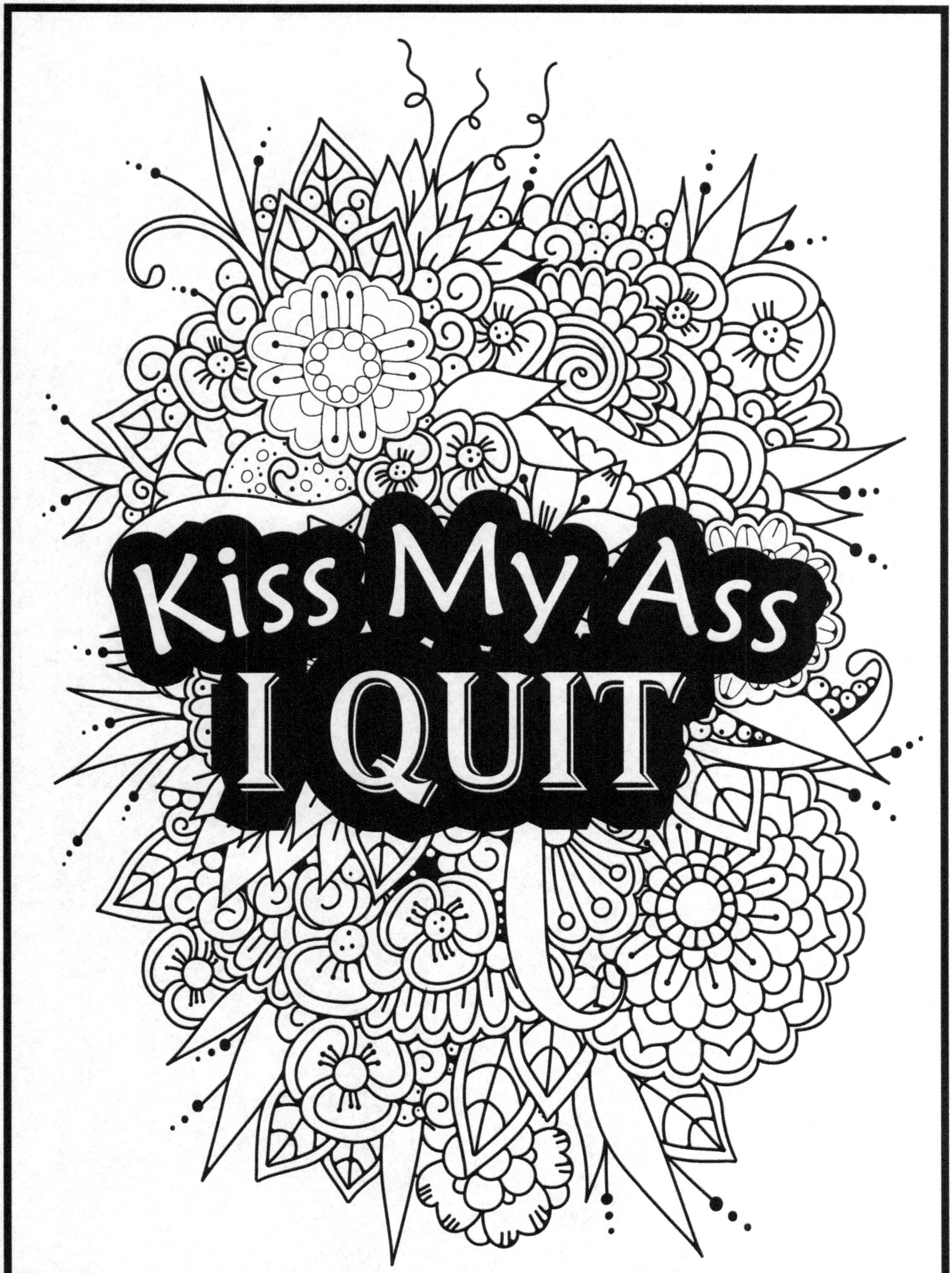
Kiss My Ass
I QUIT

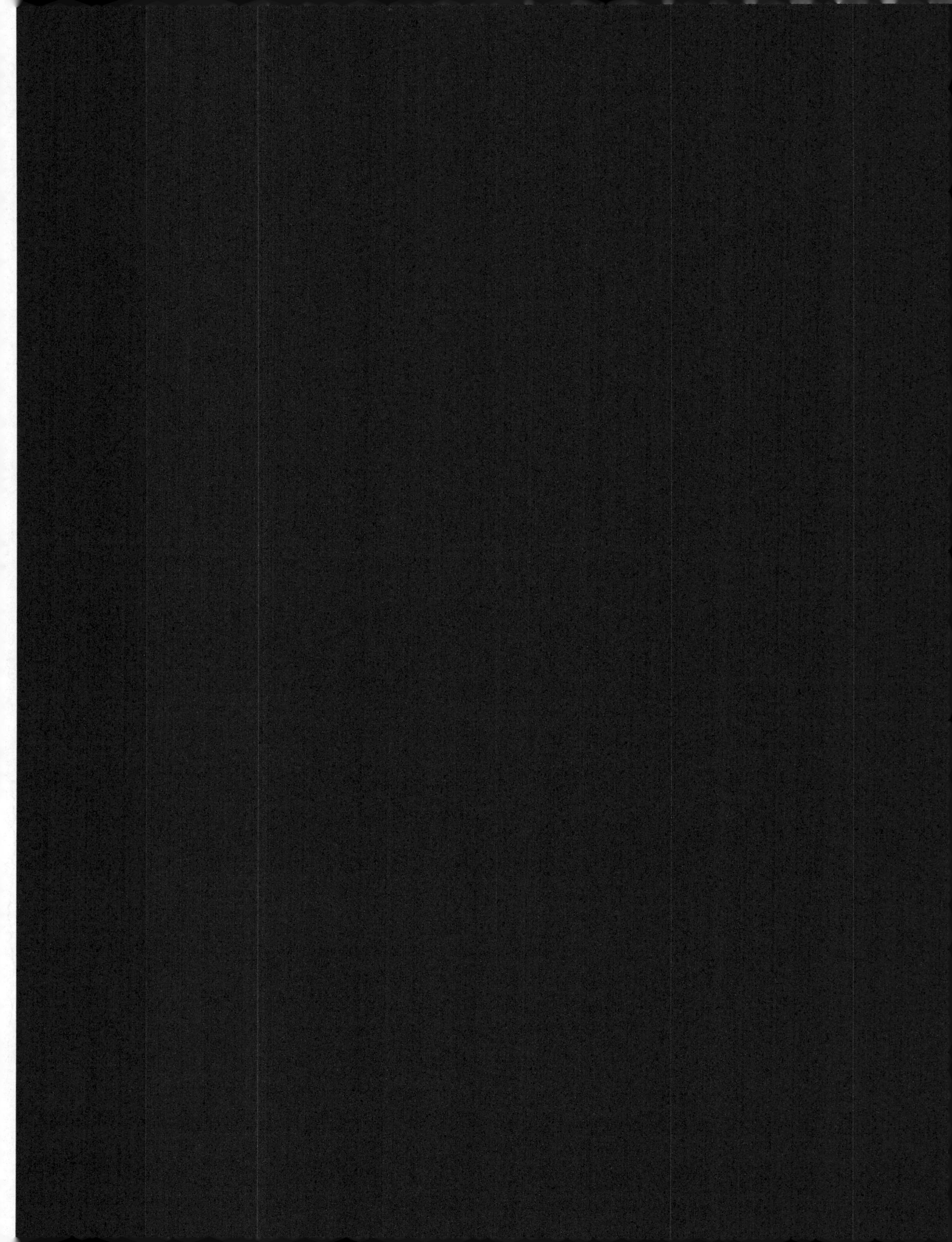

I'M CURRENTLY EXPERIENCING LIFE AT THE SPEED OF 15 WTF's PER HOUR

LOOKS LIKE IT'S F*CK THIS SH*T O'CLOCK

I HAVE PLENTY OF TALENT AND VISION I DON'T GIVE A DAMN

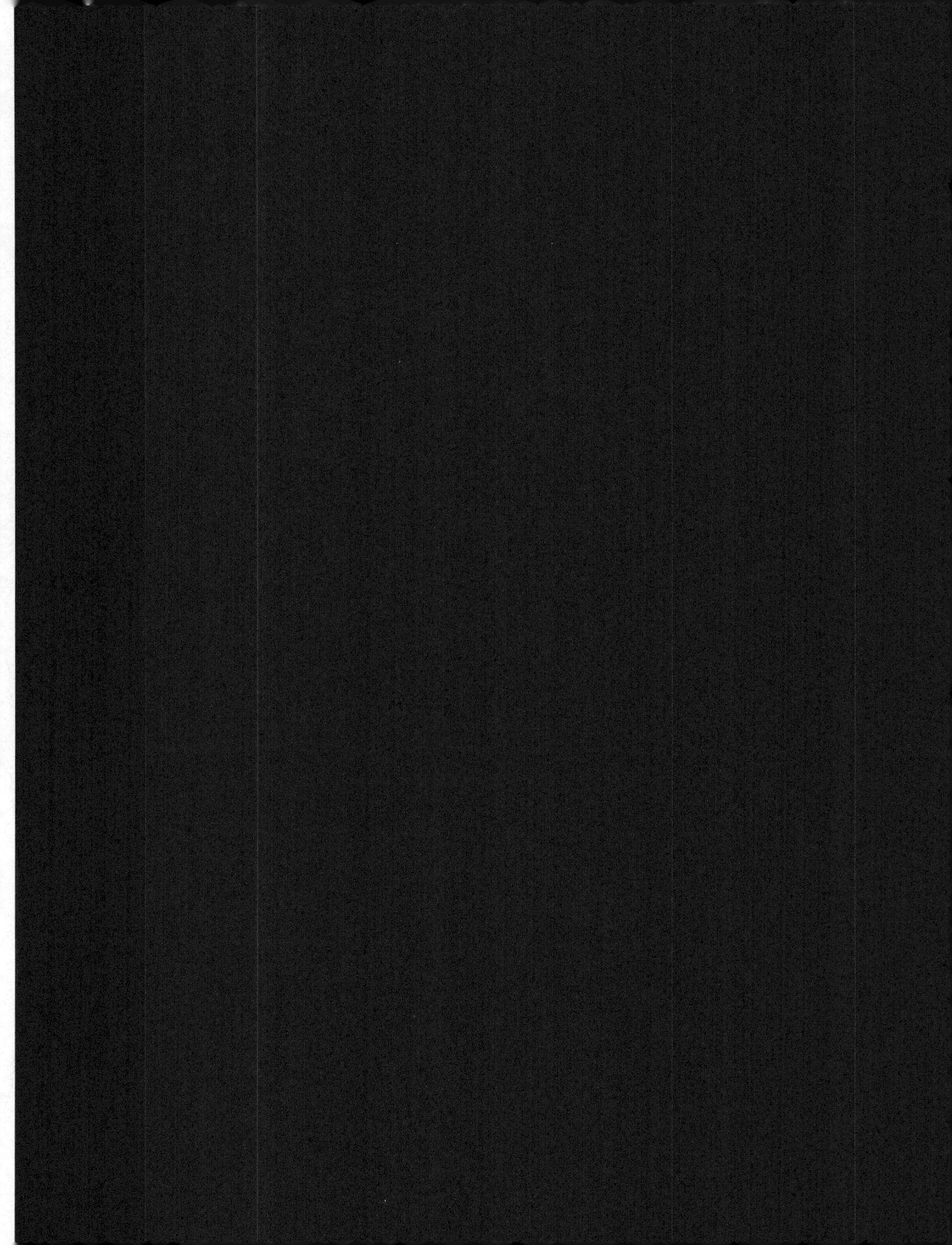

I'M TOO SOBER FOR THIS SH*T

I CAN SEE YOUR POINT BUT I STILL THINK YOU'RE FULL OF SH*T

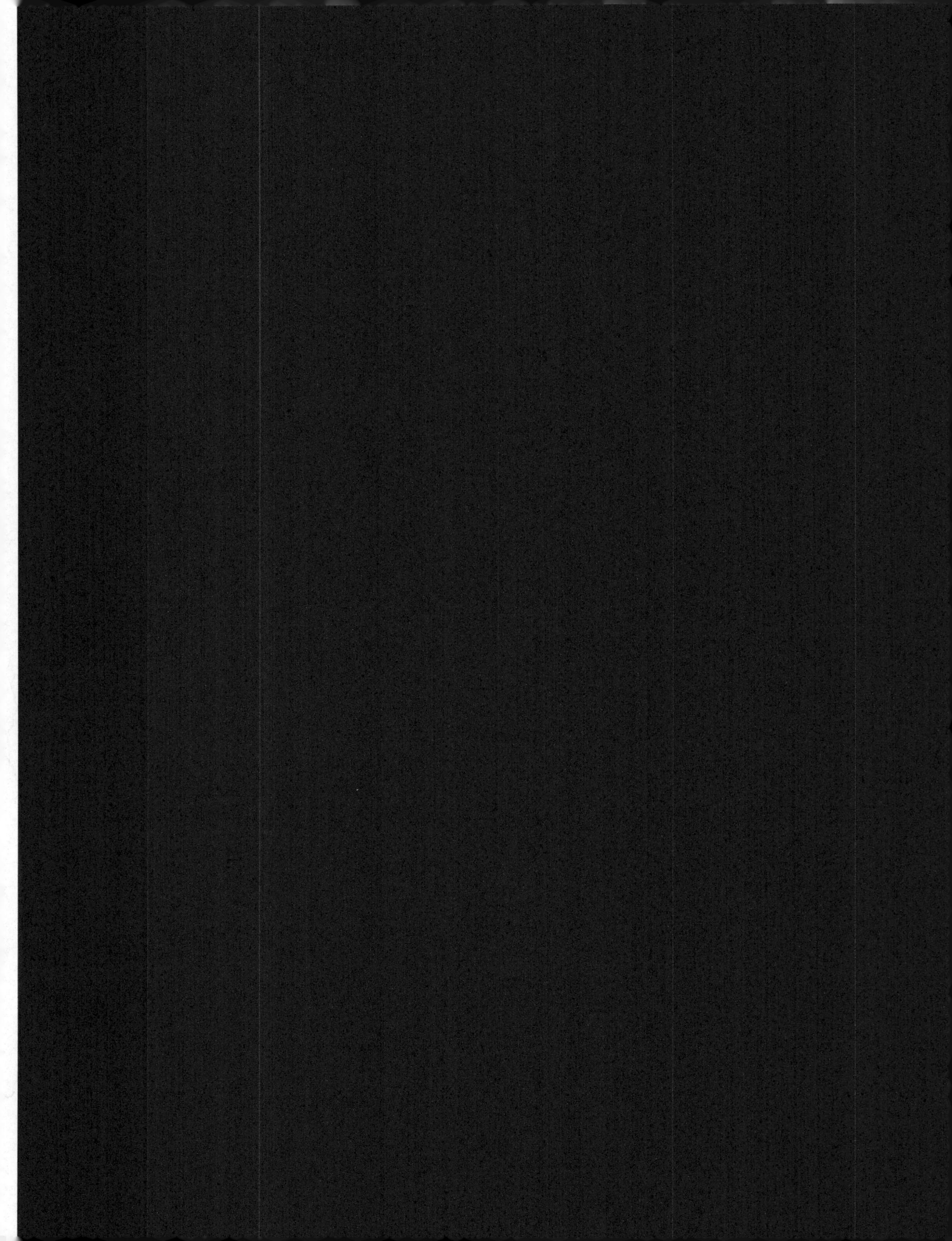

TEAMWORK IS F.*CKING OVERRATED

I'M NOT RUDE
I JUST SAY WHAT EVERYONE
ELSE IS THINKING

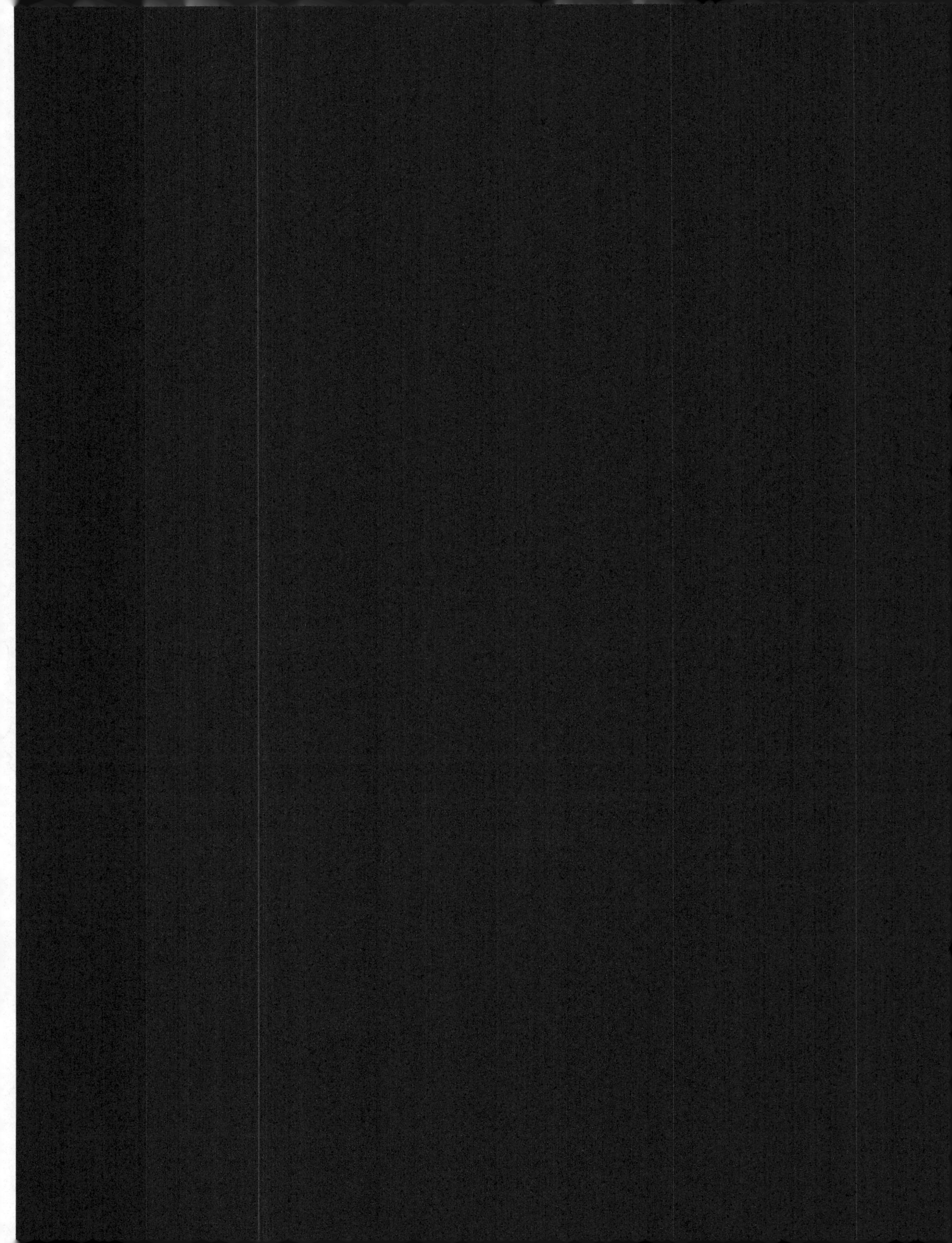

TOP OF THE MORNING TO YOU F*CKERS

Don't approach my desk unless you want a stapler up your ass

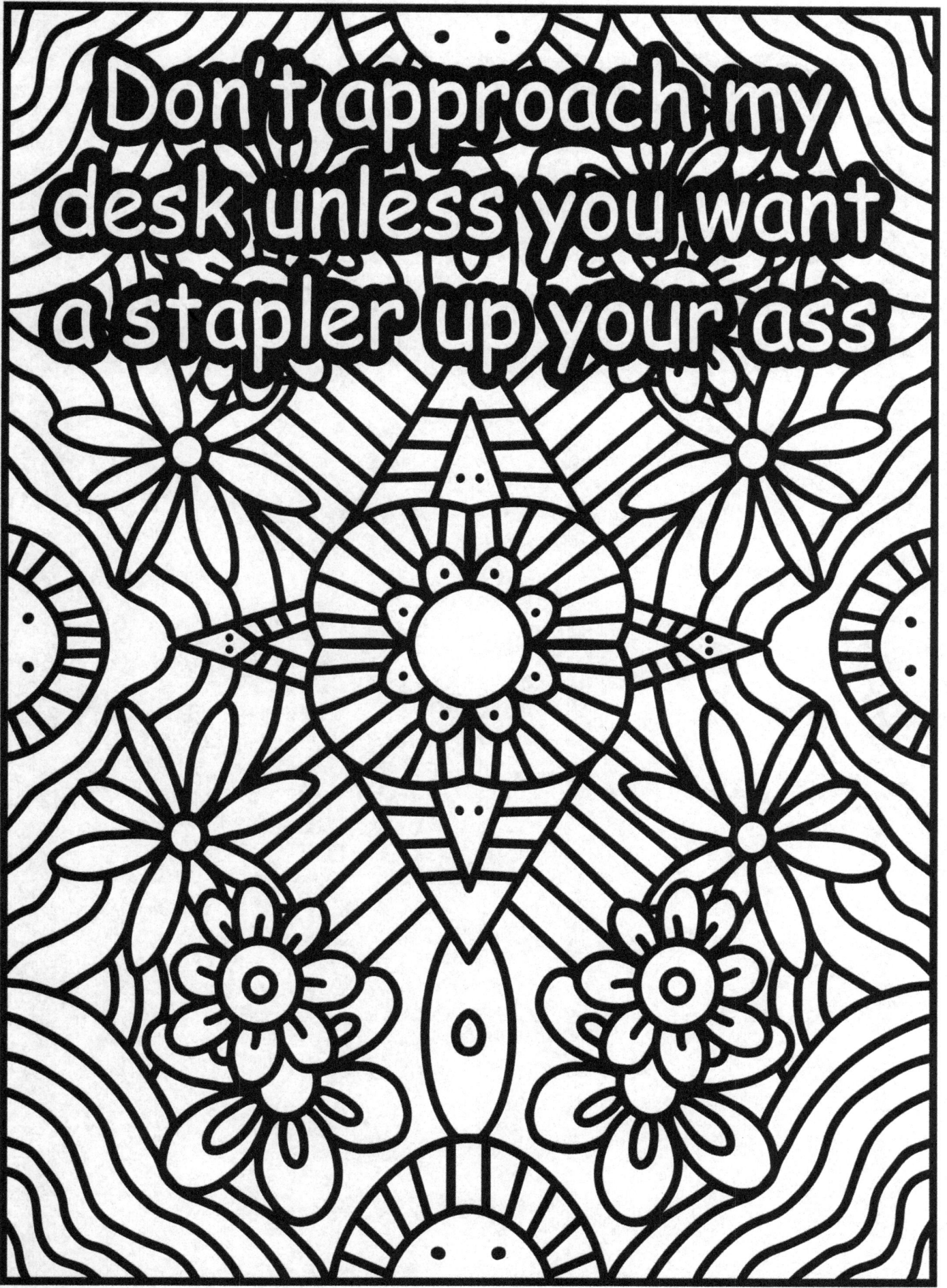

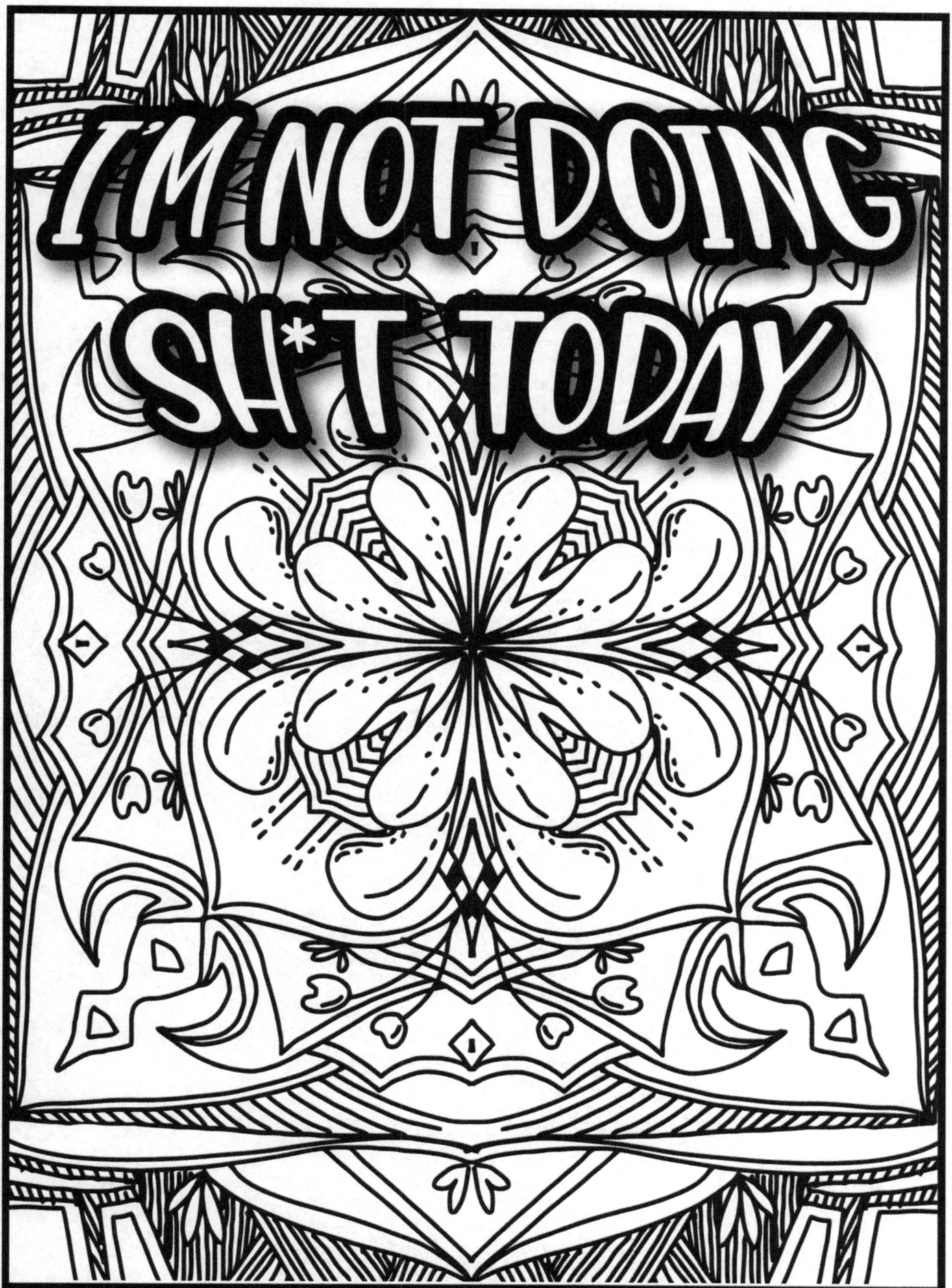

Let me put you on hold forever

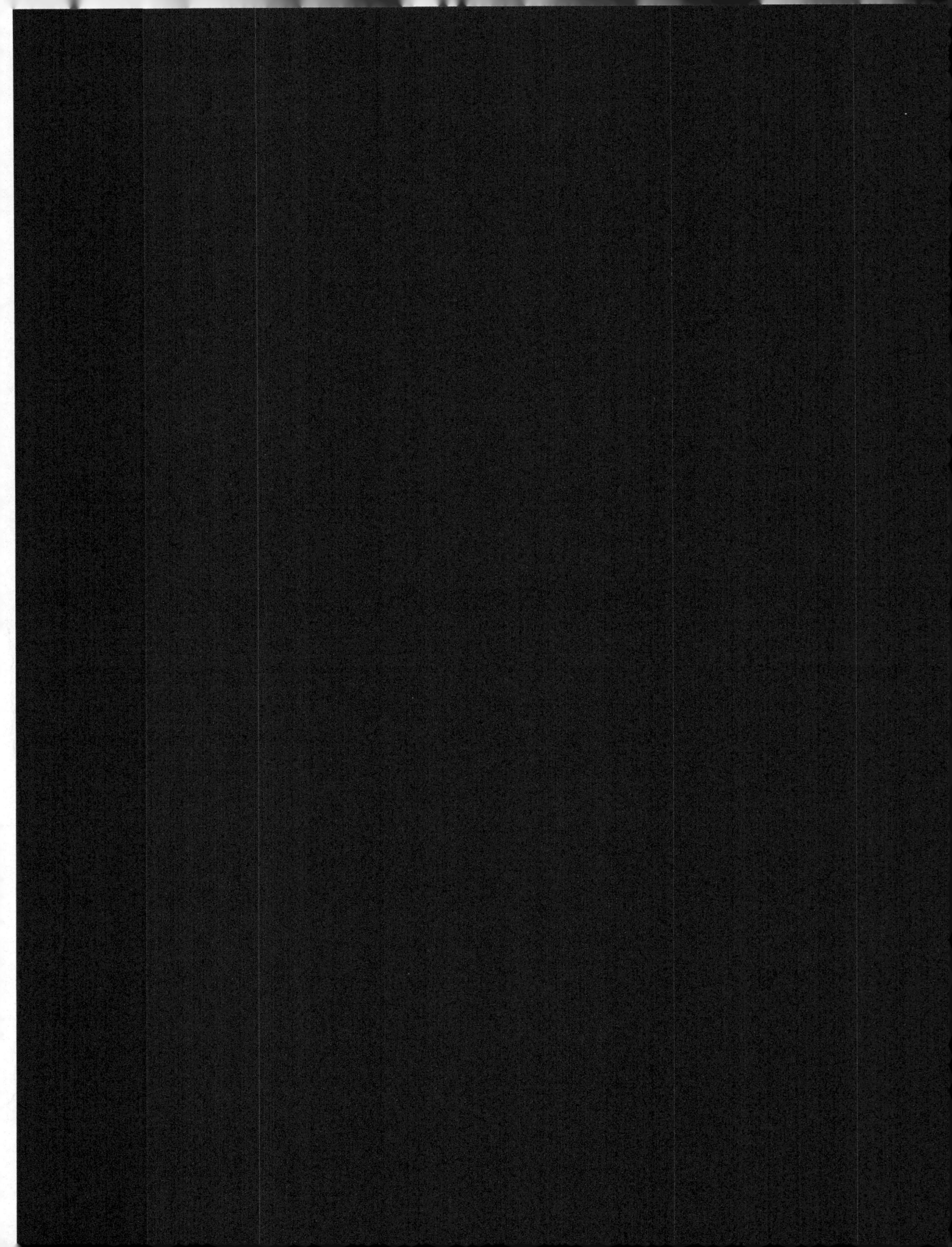

JUST ANOTHER DAY PUTTING OUT FIRES

I CAN'T BE HELD RESPONSIBLE FOR WHAT MY FACE DOES WHEN YOU TALK

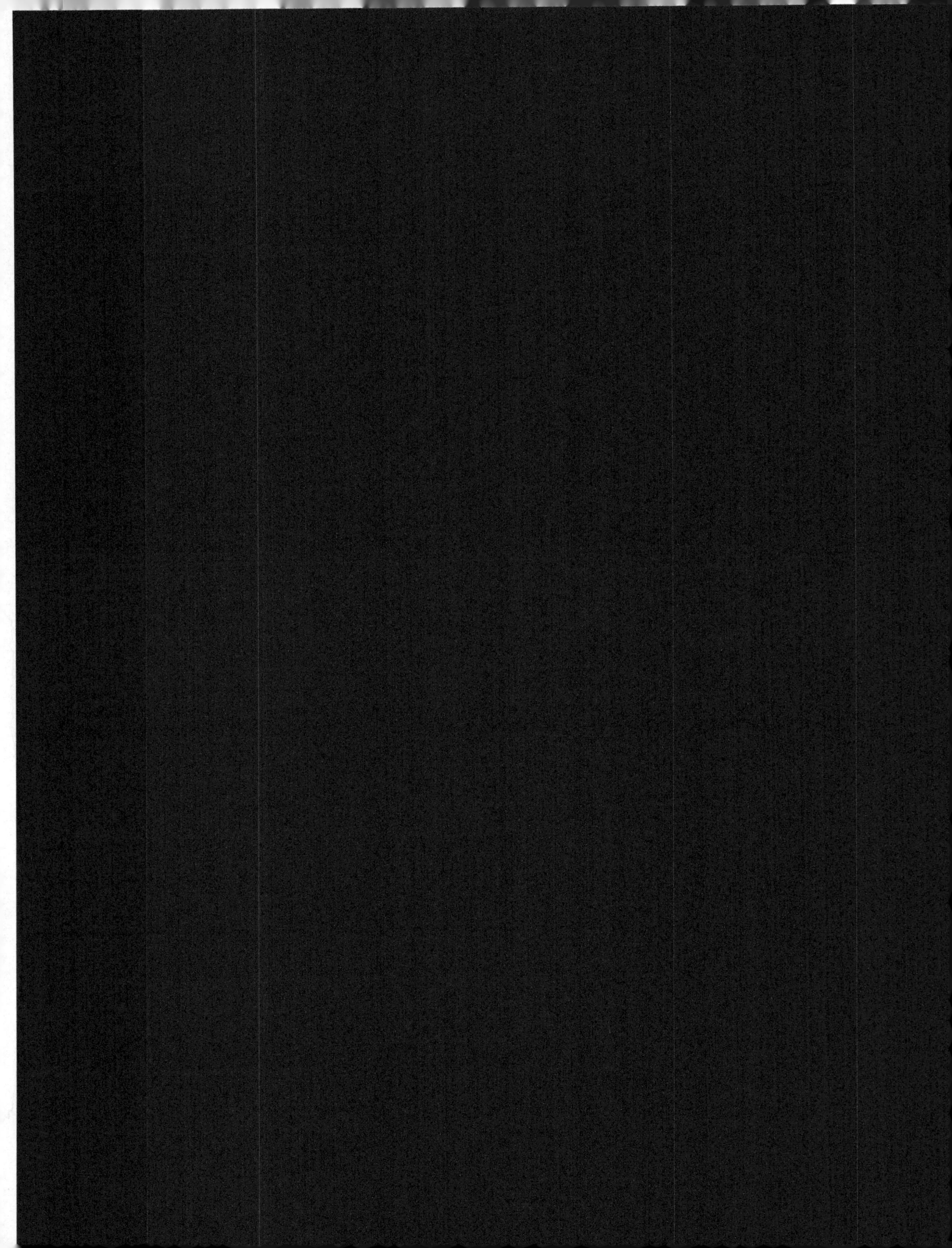

YOU SHOULD SMILE FREQUENTLY.
THE BOSS LIKE IDIOTS

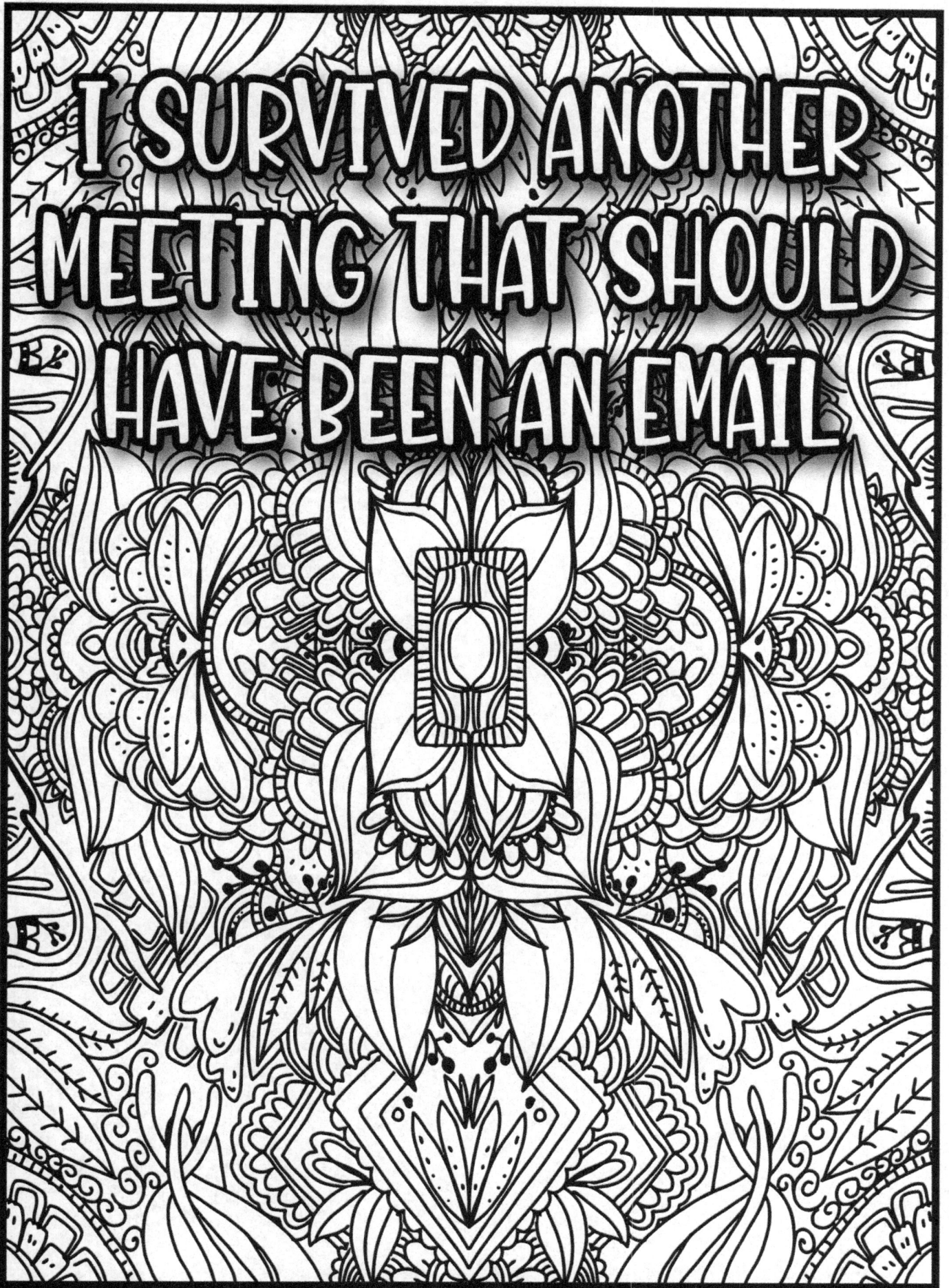
I SURVIVED ANOTHER MEETING THAT SHOULD HAVE BEEN AN EMAIL